LLES GUTE!

A guide to writing letters in German

G N Harris

Nelson

Thomas Nelson and Sons Ltd
Nelson House   Mayfield Road
Walton-on-Thames   Surrey
KT12 5PL   UK

51 York Place
Edinburgh
EH1 3JD   UK

Thomas Nelson (Hong Kong) Ltd
Toppan Building 10/F
22A Westlands Road
Quarry Bay   Hong Kong

Thomas Nelson Australia
480 La Trobe Street
Melbourne   Victoria 3000
Australia

Nelson Canada
1120 Birchmount Road
Scarborough   Ontario
M1K 5G4 Canada

© G.N. Harris 1978

First published by EJ Arnold and Son Ltd 1978
ISBN 0-560-01975-0

This edition published by Thomas Nelson and Sons Ltd 1990
ISBN 0-17-439463-2
NPN 9 8 7 6 5 4 3 2

All rights reserved. No paragraph of this publication may be reproduced, copied or transmitted save with written permission or in accordance with the provisions of the Copyright, Design and Patents Act 1988, or under the terms of any licence permitting limited copying issued by the Copyright Licencing Agency, 33-34 Alfred Place, London WC1E 7DP.

Any person who does any unauthorised act in relation to this publication may be liable to criminal prosecution and civil claims for damages.

Printed in Hong Kong

CONTENTS

With the subject matter of each letter are shown the form of address used and indications of the material selected for practice.

	Page
Introduction	4
Forms of address—starting and finishing a letter.	5

INFORMAL LETTERS

1. Introducing yourself and your family.*(Du)* — 6
   —*Setting out a letter.*
2. Describing your house.*(Du)* — 8
   —*Wie geht es?—beilegen.*
3. Describing your town or village.*(Du)* — 10
   —*Happy New Year—hoffentlich—sich erkälten.*
4. Describing your school.*(Du)* — 12
   —*Sorry I haven't written (1)—seit—mit zehn Jahren.*
5. Last year's holiday.*(Du)* — 14
   —*Sorry I haven't written (2)—Weather—*
   —*mit dem Auto—um zu.*
6. Hobbies and spare-time activities.*(Du)* — 16
   —*gern, gefallen, sich interessieren für,* etc.
7. Meeting at a station: giving instructions.*(Ihr)* — 18
   —*beim Aussteigen—Commands.*
8. Asking to be met at a station.*(Ihr)* — 19
   —*Time, Manner, Place—Asking Questions.*
9. Asking advice about a holiday.*(Du)* — 20
   —*etwas Interessantes—Holiday areas in Germany.*
10. Saying thankyou for a present.*(Du)* — 22
    —*am Londoner Flughafen—einmal am Tag.*
11. Saying thank you for hospitality.*(Sie)* — 24
    —*Spaß machen—hinauf, hinunter, entlang—*
    —*oben, unten, vorne, hinten.*
12. Cancelling arrangements.*(Sie)* — 26
    —*Relatives and family—Apologising.*
13. Wishing a happy birthday and happy Christmas.*(Du/Ihr)* — 28
    —*Expressing wishes—bei mir.*

FORMAL LETTERS

14. Requesting information from a Tourist Office.*(Sie)* — 30
    —*die Absicht haben.*
15. Reserving accommodation in a hotel.*(Sie)* — 31
    —*hiermit.*
16. Reserving a site for a tent/caravan.*(Sie)* — 32
    —*eventuell, beziehungsweise.*
17. Reserving beds in a youth hostel.*(Sie)* — 34
    —*Asking for a quick reply.*
18. Replying to an advertisement about a job.*(Sie)* — 35
    —*betrifft—beifügen—sich interessieren für.*

PRACTICE WITH EXAMINATION MATERIAL — 39

INTRODUCTION

The principal purpose of this book is to give pupils in G.C.E. and C.S.E. groups guidelines for and practice in writing letters in German. However, its usefulness is not restricted to this field. Much of the subject matter overlaps those areas of vocabulary which have to be mastered for the oral examination. In these instances, the oral and written treatment of a topic, perhaps first with the role-playing books *Geradeaus** and *Immer Weiter**, should provide valuable reinforcement, and make the writing of the letter much easier.

Each letter deals with one main topic only, to avoid distractions. The short introduction indicates the content of the letter, and the notes which follow draw the reader's attention to details such as the date, the form of address used and certain special phrases which suit particular types of letter. Difficult vocabulary is given in footnotes.

Further exploitation of each letter is arranged in sections. The first section gives relevant background information or widens a useful area of vocabulary involved in the letter. Then certain valuable linguistic constructions from a letter are taken and variations on them are offered for practice. Finally comes a section of guided exercises in writing the kind of letter with which the unit deals. Where appropriate, practice material is in the form of *Satzbautafeln* which enable all pupils to make a variety of sentences in the knowledge that they contain no mistakes. The remainder of the practice material offers something to pupils of all abilities, and the ability to select and condense material from a number of letters,

adapting and fitting it to their own requirements, should soon be within the reach of all.

Not only potential examination candidates will find this book valuable. Anyone intending to visit Germany or Austria, on holiday or on business, may need to be able to write a letter in order to reserve accommodation or to make enquiries—even to apply for a job.

My thanks go to Mr and Mrs H Reece of Worcester, and to Hartmut and Ulrike Kindermann of Münster, for their help in supplying some of the support material and in revising the work. I am grateful to Pauline Robinson of Upton-on-Severn for the delightful drawings, and to the various Examining Boards for their cooperation in allowing me to use certain questions from their past papers.

G N Harris.
Eckington, 1978

*Geradeaus. German Situational Dialogues
Book 1 ISBN 0 560 01970 X
*Immer Weiter. German Situational Dialogues
Book 2 ISBN 0 560 01971 8
Both books published by Arnold-Wheaton

FORMS OF ADDRESS

This table will enable you to begin and end your letters correctly. When you have decided which type of letter you are writing, use the material from the appropriate line. All the German words for 'you', 'your', etc. must be written with a capital, including *Du* and *Ihr*, when they are in a letter to someone.

Type of letter	Dear	You (subject)	You (object)	You (dative)	Your	Command	Signing off	Yours (ending)
INFORMAL one person	Lieber Hans! Liebe Erika!	Du	Dich	Dir	Dein	schreib	viele Grüße; es grüßt Dich herzlich; herzliche Grüße; alles Gute; mit herzlichen Grüßen	Dein *or* Deine
INFORMAL two/more people	Liebe Eva, lieber Werner!	Ihr	Euch	Euch	Euer	schreibt	as above, except: es grüßt Euch herzlich; herzliche Grüße Euch allen	Euer *or* Eure
FORMAL singular or plural	Lieber Herr M! Liebe Frau M! Sehr geehrter Herr! Sehr geehrte Herren!	Sie	Sie	Ihnen	Ihr	schreiben Sie	Hochachtungsvoll	Ihr *or* Ihre

INFORMAL LETTERS

This could be the first letter to a new penfriend. In it, you explain how you got your penfriend's address, introduce yourself and say a little about your family and where you live.

Lieber Rolf!

Appledore, den 12. Januar

Ich bekam Deine Adresse von meinem Deutschlehrer. Es würde mir Freude machen, einen Briefwechsel mit Dir beginnen zu können.

Zuerst muß ich mich vorstellen. Ich heiße John Taylor und bin fünfzehn Jahre alt. Ich habe am ersten März Geburtstag. Ich habe einen siebzehnjährigen Bruder, der Stephen heißt, und eine Schwester Alison, die zwölf Jahre alt ist. Wir wohnen in einem Einfamilienhaus in Appledore, einer kleinen Stadt im Südwesten von England. Mein Vater ist Tierarzt* und arbeitet teils in der Stadt, teils auf dem Lande. Mutter ist eigentlich Hausfrau aber sie hilft Vater in den Sprechstunden.

In dem nächsten Brief werde ich Dir etwas über unser Haus schreiben.

Viele Grüße, auch an Deine Eltern,

Dein

John.

Points to notice:
(a) The date on German letters is always written: *den* + number + full stop + month.
(b) Germans put only the town at the top of a letter. Their full address appears on the back of the envelope after *Absender*.
(c) The exclamation mark after the name of the person you are writing to.
(d) *Du, Dein*, etc. are written with capitals in letters.

*Tierarzt—*vet.*

A I *You can work out the correct permutation for your family by using the table.*

Ich habe	einen eine keinen keine zwei	Bruder Brüder Schwester Schwestern Geschwister

II *Which one do you live in?*

Wir wohnen in einem Doppelhaus/in einem Einfamilienhaus/in einem Reihenhaus/in einem Bungalow/in einer Wohnung/auf einem Bauernhof.

III *Notice that when you are talking about someone's job, you do not use* ein. *You say, for example:*

Mein Vater ist Mechaniker, mein Bruder ist Student, meine Schwester ist Sekretärin, meine Mutter ist Krankenschwester.

MEIN VATER IST ARBEITSLOS.

IV *When you write a letter introducing yourself, you may need to use some of this vocabulary:*

die Organisation	im Norden
die Großstadt (¨e)	im Süden
das Dorf (¨er)	im Osten
auf dem Lande	im Westen
in der Mitte von England	im Nordosten
in der Nähe von	im Nordwesten
tot — *dead*	im Südosten
geschieden — *divorced*	im Südwesten

B I *Answer these questions from a penfriend's letter:*

1 Möchtest du einen Briefwechsel mit mir beginnen?
2 Wie alt bist du?
3 Hast du Geschwister?
4 Wo wohnst du?
5 Was macht dein Vater?
6 Arbeitet deine Mutter?

II *See if you can ask your new penfriend a few questions about himself or herself:*

1 Ask his or her age.
2 Ask how old his/her brother/sister is.
3 Ask what father's job is.

III *Write a short letter to a new penfriend:*

1 Say you got the letter from an organisation.
2 You would like to start corresponding.
3 Introduce yourself and your family, saying where you live.
4 Offer your best wishes to your friend's parents.

2 *This letter contains a simple description of where you live. It also helps you to ask how someone is, and to say that you are enclosing something with the letter.*

Liebe Karin!

Burslem, den 1. Februar

Vielen Dank für Deinen netten Brief. Wie geht es Dir und Deiner Familie? Uns geht es gut.

Zunächst ein paar Zeilen über unser Haus. Wie gesagt, wohnen wir in einem mittelgroßen Einfamilienhaus am Rande der Stadt. Oben haben wir vier Schlafzimmer und das Badezimmer, und unten sind die Küche, das Wohnzimmer, das Eßzimmer und eine Toilette mit einer Dusche.

Vor und hinter dem Haus haben wir einen Garten; vorne sind Rosen und hinten ist ein Rasen. Wir bauen auch etwas Gemüse an. Ich lege Dir ein Foto von unserem Haus bei.

Bitte, schreib bald wieder!

Es grüßt Dich herzlich

Deine,

Lynn.

Points to notice:
(a) This time, a girl is writing to another girl. Notice the different form of *Liebe* at the beginning and *Deine* at the end.
(b) There is a different way of signing off. See how many different ways of ending an informal letter are used in this book.

A I *With these tables you can easily ask how people are, and say how you are in reply:*

Wie geht es	Deinem Deiner Deinen Eurem Eurer Euren Ihrem Ihrer Ihren	Vater? Mutter? Eltern? Familie?
Danke,	mir ihr ihm ihnen uns allen	geht es gut.

II *Find the phrase which describes where you live:*

Wir wohnen mitten in der Stadt/in einem Vorort/ außerhalb der Stadt/in einem Dorf/auf dem Lande/ am Rande der Stadt.

B I *Say you enclose the following things:*

1 a photo of your house.
2 a photo of your family.
3 a postcard of the town.
4 a town plan.
5 some English stamps.

II *Include the following points in a letter to a penfriend:*

1 Say thankyou for the letter.
2 Ask how his or her parents are.
3 Say your family is well.
4 Briefly describe your house.
5 Briefly describe your garden.
6 Say you enclose a photo of yourself.

III *A few variations:*

1 Say thankyou for the letter.
2 Ask how he or she is.
3 Say you are all right.
4 Describe your own room, or your living-room.
5 Say you enclose a photo of your family.

This letter shows how you can describe the town or village where you live. It revises how to thank someone for their letter, and how to ask about someone's health.

Cropthorne, den 31. Dezember

Lieber Gerd!

Recht vielen Dank für Deinen letzten Brief. Hoffentlich geht es Deinem Vater besser. Mutti hat sich auch schwer erkältet.

Cropthorne ist ein kleines Dorf, das zwischen Pershore und Evesham an dem Fluß Avon liegt. Kannst Du es auf der Landkarte finden? Es gibt etwa 500 Einwohner. Wir haben ein Postamt, wo man auch Lebensmittel kaufen kann, und zwei Wirtshäuser. Die Kirche ist alt und sehr schön, und gibt nicht viel für junge Leute. Wenn man ins Kino gehen will, muß man nach Evesham oder Worcester fahren. In Pershore ist ein modernes Hallenbad, und in Worcester sind sehr gute, große Geschäfte. Aber auf dem Lande fahren die Autobusse nicht sehr oft, und das macht Schwierigkeiten, wenn man in eine Diskothek gehen will.

Ich wohne gern hier. Es ist ruhig und im Sommer ist es besonders schön. Ich lege Dir zwei Ansichtskarten von dem Dorf bei.

Herzliche Grüße Euch allen, und ein glückliches Neues Jahr.

Dein,

Notice: A third way of signing off a letter to a friend, and this time you are sending your good wishes to all the family.

A I *Your own town or village could lie:*

an einem Fluß (an der Themse), an der See *or* an der Küste, an einem See, in der Nähe von der See.

II *Here are the names of a few places you could use if you are describing a town:*

das Schwimmbad (Hallenbad)
der Tennisplatz
der Kinderspielplatz
der Zoo/der Tierpark
das Theater
der Dom—*cathedral*
die Universität
die Gemäldegalerie—*picture gallery*
der Park
die Kegelbahn—*bowling alley*
das Museum
die Abtei—*abbey*

B I *Practise using* hoffentlich:

1 I hope your mother is better.
2 I hope your family is well.
3 I hope you are all right.

II *Practise using* sich erkälten *(to catch a cold). Remember this is a reflexive verb, and that you have to keep to this pattern:*

with:	ich	use:	mich
	du		dich
	er, sie, es		sich
	wir		uns
	ihr		euch
	sie, Sie		sich

1 Father has caught a cold.
2 I have caught a cold.
3 Have you caught a cold?

C *Write a short letter to Gerd:*

1 Thank him for his last letter.
2 Say you hope he is well.
3 Say you have caught a cold.
4 Briefly describe the town or village where you live.
5 Say if you like or dislike where you live.
6 Say you enclose some postcards.

4 *This letter shows how you can describe your school and what you do there. It also suggests a useful way of apologising for not having written, which you will probably need sooner or later!*

Liebe Helga!

Derby, den 8. April

Es tut mir leid, daß ich so lange nicht geschrieben habe. Wir haben gerade unsere Prüfungen gemacht, und ich bin nicht zum Schreiben gekommen.

Ich habe Dir noch nichts über meine Schule geschrieben. Ich besuche eine Gesamtschule mit etwa 1200 Schülern und Schülerinnen. Die Schule fängt um 9 Uhr an und ist um zehn vor vier aus. Wir haben eine kleine Pause um viertel vor elf, und die meisten Kinder essen zu Mittag in der Schule. Ich bin in der vierten Klasse. Englisch und Mathematik sind Pflichtfächer,* und man kann noch fünf andere Fächer wählen. Meine Lieblingsfächer sind die Fremdsprachen, Französisch und Deutsch, und ich studiere auch Geschichte gern. Ich studiere Biologie schon seit drei Jahren. Mit sechzehn Jahren macht man Prüfungen (O Levels oder CSE), und ich werde dann in der sechsten Klasse weiterstudieren.

Meine Klassenkameraden und ich meinen, daß wir zu viele Hausaufgaben haben! Ich lege Dir meinen Stundenplan bei.

Alles Gute,

Deine
Christine

*Pflichtfächer —*compulsory subjects.*

Notice: Another new way of finishing a letter to a friend, and a useful phrase in its own right.

A *What kind of school do you go to? Is it among these?*

eine Gesamtschule (gemischte; für Jungen; für Mädchen); ein Gymnasium, eine Realschule, ein Internat.

B I *You can see in the letter how to say "I have been studying Biology for three years" using* seit.
Practise using seit:

1 I have been studying German for three years.
2 I have been doing history for five years.
3 I have been doing geography for four years.

II *Now answer these questions using* seit:

1 Seit wann studierst du Französisch?
2 Seit wann studierst du Physik?
3 Seit wann studierst du Deutsch?

III *Find in the letter one way of saying "at the age of sixteen". Using this construction, put in the correct age at the beginning of each sentence:*

1 ... geht man in die Grundschule.
2 ... geht man in eine Gesamtschule.
3 ... macht man die "O" Level Prüfungen.
4 ... macht man das Abitur in Deutschland.
5 ... macht man den Führerschein.

IV *Try to answer these questions about your school day:*
1 Wieviele Stunden hast du jeden Tag?
2 Wieviele Stunden Deutsch hast du in der Woche?
3 Was ist dein Lieblingsfach?
4 Wie lange dauert die Mittagspause bei dir?
5 In welcher Klasse bist du?
6 Was sind deine Pflichtfächer?
7 Seit wann studierst du Englisch?
8 Kommst du gern in die Schule?
9 Was gefällt dir am besten in der Schule? *Oder:* Warum kommst du nicht gern in die Schule?
10 Wie kommst du in die Schule?

C *Practise writing a letter to your penfriend about your school:*

1 Apologise for not having written.
2 Ask how he or she is.
3 Briefly describe your school.
4 Ask what his/her favourite subject is.
5 Ask how long he/she has been learning English.
6 Say you enclose your timetable.

5

This letter deals with a holiday which you have already spent. There is another way of apologising for not having written and revision of asking after someone.

—WIR SIND SKIGELAUFEN......

Points to notice:
(a) Yet another way of signing off an informal letter.
(b) At the end you can see how to ask someone to write back soon.

Exeter, den 21. Mai

Lieber Gerd!

 Es ist nun schon vier Wochen her, seit ich von mir hören ließ. Entschuldige, bitte, daß ich so lange nicht geschrieben habe. Wie geht es Dir und Deiner Familie?

 Wir wollen dieses Jahr unsere Ferien in Deutschland verbringen. Im Winter sind wir auch ins Ausland gefahren, und zwar* nach Österreich. Wir sind mit dem Zug nach Innsbruck gefahren und haben zwei Wochen da verbracht. Es war prima! Meine Eltern sind Ski gelaufen und wir sind alle Schlittschuh gelaufen*. Dann haben wir einen zweitägigen Ausflug nach Wien gemacht. Wir haben da eine Stadtrundfahrt gemacht, um die Sehenswürdigkeiten zu sehen, dann mußten wir Einkäufe machen, um Souvenirs zu kaufen. Am zweiten Tag haben wir Schloß Schönbrunn besichtigt und den Prater besucht. Warst Du schon einmal in Wien?

 Das Wetter war schön—kalt aber sonnig. Das Essen hat mir wirklich gut geschmeckt und die Ferien haben mir besonders gut gefallen.

 Schreib bald wieder. Herzliche Grüße,
    Dein,
    Richard.

*und zwar = *to be precise*. A common phrase which you will find again in later letters. It is used more in German than 'to be precise' is used in English.
*Schlittschuh laufen = *to skate*.

A I *If you go on holiday to a town, use* nach:

nach Bournemouth, nach London, nach Berlin.

For most countries we use nach *as well*:
nach Italien, nach Frankreich, nach Spanien.

But some are different, because they are feminine or plural:
Wir fahren in die Schweiz; wir waren in den Vereinigten Staaten.

Remember: Wir fahren ins Ausland; wir waren im Ausland.

II *These are the commonest ways of describing the weather*:

Es war schön, warm, kalt, nebelig, sonnig, windig, naß. Die Sonne scheint (schien), es regnet (regnete), es schneit (schneite), es donnert (donnerte), es blitzt (blitzte).

III *You may find these phrases useful for describing what you did on holiday*:

einen Ausflug		Ski laufen
einen Spaziergang		rodeln — *to sledge*
ein Picknick	machen	schwimmen, baden
Einkäufe		wandern
eine Rundfahrt		die Sehenswürdigkeiten
eine Besichtigung		besichtigen

IV *How did you get there?*

mit dem Zug, mit dem Auto (Wagen), mit dem Boot, mit dem Schiff, mit dem Flugzeug, mit dem Rad, mit dem Roller, mit der Bahn, mit der Fähre, mit der Straßenbahn, eventuell mit dem Hubschrauber, zu Fuß!

B *Practise using* um zu, *a very important construction.*

Example: Wir sind nach Wien gefahren und haben einen Ausflug gemacht.
Wir sind nach Wien gefahren, um einen Ausflug zu machen.

Now change the following sentences in the same way:
1 Wir sind nach Wien gefahren und haben Einkäufe gemacht.
2 Wir sind in den Wald gegangen und haben einen Spaziergang gemacht.
3 Wir sind auf das Land gegangen und haben ein Picknick gemacht.
4 Wir haben eine Rundfahrt gemacht und haben die Sehenswürdigkeiten gesehen.
5 Wir sind nach Wien gefahren und haben Schloß Schönbrunn besichtigt.
6 Wir sind nach Innsbruck gefahren und sind Ski gelaufen.
7 Wir sind nach Innsbruck gefahren und sind Schlittschuh gelaufen.

C I *Practise writing a letter to Gerd about a recent holiday*:

1 Apologise for not having written for so long.
2 Ask how he is.
3 Describe a recent holiday.
4 Say what the weather was like.
5 Say if you enjoyed the food and the holiday.

II *Now reply to the following points Gerd raised in his last letter*:

1 Wo hast du letztes Jahre deine Ferien verbracht?
2 Was hast du dort gemacht?
3 Wie war das Wetter?
4 Wie hat es dir dort gefallen?

6

This time hobbies and spare-time activities are covered. Don't forget that a good letter will not only give the reader information, it will also ask a few questions.

Fleetwood, den 30. Juni

Liebe Eva!

Gott sei Dank, daß das Wochenende wieder da ist, und daß ich mit meinen ewigen Schularbeiten fertig bin! Ich würde mich freuen, wenn ich nachmittags keine Schule hätte. Du hast es wirklich gut!

Jedes Wochenende arbeiten mein Bruder und ich halbtags, um etwas Geld zu verdienen. Samstagmorgens arbeite ich als Verkäuferin in einem großen Kaufhaus, und Brian verkauft Benzin in einer Tankstelle. Mit dem Geld, das ich verdiene, kaufe ich Schallplatten und Kleider. Ich interessiere mich natürlich für Popmusik. Hast Du eine Lieblingsgruppe? Ich bin ein Fan von Black Sabbath. Ich sammele nichts, weder Briefmarken noch Münzen, aber ich lese gern. Bücher über Tiere gefallen mir. Treibst Du gern Sport? Ich habe keine Lust dazu, aber ich sehe manchmal Fußball im Fernsehen. Siehst Du viel fern? Ungefähr einmal im Monat gehe ich zur Disco oder zu einer Party, und ich gehe auch ins Kino, wenn ein guter Film läuft. Ich habe keine Lust, ins Theater zu gehen. Sonntags gehen wir in die Kirche, und nachher besuchen wir ab und zu Verwandte. Das finde ich ziemlich langweilig.

Jetzt muß ich Schluß machen. Ich lege Dir ein Bild von Black Sabbath bei. Sind sie in Deutschland bekannt? Schreib bald.

Viele Grüße,
Deine,

Ann

A I *You will find it easier to say what you do at weekends, and what your hobbies are if you use this table:*

Ich	spiele	gern lieber nicht gern am liebsten oft nicht oft	Fußball Tennis Federball
	höre		klassische Musik Popmusik allerlei Musik Schallplatten
	mache		Ausflüge Spaziergänge Einkäufe
	gehe		ins Kino ins Theater schwimmen

II *Here are some more useful phrases to do with hobbies and spare time activities:*

halbtags arbeiten — *to work part-time*
sich interessieren für *(Acc)* — *to be interested in*
sammeln (sammelte) — *to collect*
gern + haben *or another infinitive* — *to like*
(Sport) treiben — *to go in for (sport)*
(keine) Lust haben zu — *(not) to feel like*
fernsehen (sah fern) — *to watch television*
im Fernsehen — *on TV*
Filme/Bücher/Programme über *(Acc)* — *films/books/programmes about*
einmal im Monat — *once a month*
einmal in der Woche — *once a week*
gefallen (gefiel) *(Dat.)* — *to appeal to*

B I *Here are five linked phrases which express an interest in, or a liking for something — in this case the cinema or films:*

Ich interessiere mich für Filme.
Ich habe kein Interesse an Filmen. *(not interested in)*
Ich gehe gern ins Kino.
Das Kino gefällt mir. (Filme gefallen mir).
Ich habe Lust, ins Kino zu gehen.

II *Now try to use the five constructions with each of these pastimes:*

1 Bücher   4 Programme über Sport
2 Fußball   5 Popmusik *oder* klassische Musik
3 Discos   6 Zeichnen

By using nicht *or a form of* kein *you can easily say that you dislike some of these pastimes.*

C I *You have received a letter asking you some questions about yourself. Write your reply. Here are the questions:*

1 Was machst du am Wochenende?
2 Interessierst du dich für Popmusik?
3 Hast du eine Lieblingsgruppe?
4 Sammelst du etwas.
5 Treibst du gern Sport?
6 Siehst du viel fern?
7 Was für Programme, beziehungsweise Filme, siehst du am liebsten?

II *Practise writing a letter to Eva about what you do at the weekend, and how your leisure time is spent:*

1 Say you are glad that the weekend has come, and that you have finished your homework.
2 Say what you do on most weekends, and describe generally what your hobbies are.
3 Say you have to finish.
4 Say you enclose a picture of your favourite group

This letter gives instructions about where someone is to wait so that you can come and meet them.

Gillingham, den 9. Juli

Liebe Ingrid, lieber Werner!

Danke für Euren Brief. Es freut uns, daß Ihr uns endlich besucht. Wir werden Euch von dem Liverpool Street Bahnhof abholen.

Euer Zug kommt um halb vier in Liverpool Street an. Beim Aussteigen werdet Ihr eine große Uhr sehen. Wartet auf uns unter dieser Uhr. Ihr werdet mich sicher von den Fotos erkennen, aber ich werde einen roten Pullover und einen weißen Schal tragen, damit Ihr mich nicht verpaßt. Wir werden dann gleich nach Hause fahren und etwas zu essen haben.

Hoffentlich werdet Ihr eine gute Reise haben. Ich freue mich schon auf den zwanzigsten — bis dann!

Einen schönen Gruß an Eure Eltern,
Eure,
Louise.

Notice: An important change in the form of address. We are now writing to two friends, and this involves:
(a) The appropriate forms of *Lieber* at the beginning, one for each of the people you are writing to.
(b) The change of *Du-Dich-Dir-Dein* to *Ihr-Euch-Euch-Euer*.
(c) A different way of saying "yours" at the end.

A *Here are a few landmarks at a station:*

der Zeitungsstand — *newspaper stall*
die Gepäckaufbewahrung — *left luggage office*
die Sperre — *barrier*
der Fahrplan — *timetable*

B I *Notice the construction "on getting out" or "when you get out"*: beim Aussteigen. *Make similar phrases for:*
1 when playing football   4 when skiing
2 when swimming   5 at mealtime(s).
3 when getting in

II *When making arrangements it is often necessary to give commands. Here are two examples, the first a weak verb, the second a strong verb:*
(a) wait for me: wart(e) auf mich/wartet auf mich/warten Sie auf mich.
(b) give me: gib mir/gebt mir/geben Sie mir.

Now practise the 3 different forms of each of these:
1 Come with me.   2 Look.   3 Help me.
4 Read.   5 Stop.   6 Tell.

C *Practise writing a letter to two friends — a brother and a sister who have just written to say that they are coming to visit you:*

1 Thank them for their letter.
2 Say you are glad that they can visit you.
3 Say you will meet them at the station.
4 Tell them where to wait on the station, and say how they can recognise you easily.
5 Say you hope they have a good journey, and that you are looking forward to when they arrive.

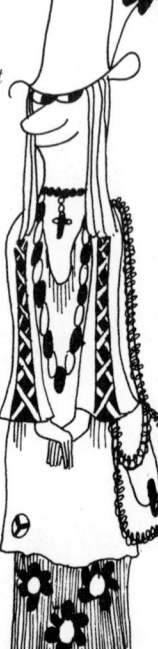

—DAMIT DU MICH ERKENNEN KANNST....

This letter confirms the date, time and place of your arrival in Germany, and asks if your friends can meet you.

Hereford, den 7. August.

Liebe Familie Hoffmann!

Vielen Dank für Euren letzten Brief. Wie geht es Euch? Ich habe einen Schnupfen gehabt, aber sonst geht es gut.

Der Deutschlandbesuch steht jetzt fest. Ich komme um zehn nach zwei am einundzwanzigsten August mit dem Zug in Köln an. Könnt Ihr mich von dem Bahnhof abholen? Bitte, sagt mir, wo ich auf Euch warten soll. Ich lege Euch das neueste Foto von mir bei, damit Ihr mich erkennen könnt.

Ich freue mich schon auf den Besuch. Hoffentlich klappt alles! Bis bald.

Herzliche Grüße,
Euer,
Mark.

A It is important to remember word order in a German sentence. One aspect of this is:

Time — Manner — Place

When *something happens* goes before *how it happens*, which goes before *where it happens*. Thus:
Der Zug kommt um zehn Uhr in Köln an.
Ich fahre jeden Tag mit dem Bus in die Schule.

German sentences often begin with Time:
Jeden Tag fahre ich mit dem Bus in die Stadt.

B *You can see how to ask the family if they can meet you:*
Könnt ihr mich von dem Bahnhof abholen?

Now ask the same question of:

1 Werner.
2 Herr Schäfer.
3 Herr und Frau Weber.
4 Werner und Sabine.

C I *Practise writing a letter to the family about your visit:*

1 Thank them for their last letter and ask how they are.
2 Say you have had a cold but are all right apart from that.
3 Give details about when and where your train will arrive.
4 Ask if they can meet you, and to tell you where you should wait for them.
5 Say you enclose the latest photo of yourself so that they can recognise you.
6 Say you are looking forward to the visit and that you hope everything goes well.

II *Werner is coming to visit you, and has written giving details. Write back, making the following points:*

1 Thank him for the letter and photograph.
2 Say you are looking forward to his visit.
3 Say you can meet him at the station, and tell him where to wait for you.
4 Wish him a good journey (page 18) and say you will see him soon.

In this letter you ask advice about a proposed holiday in Germany and suggest that you might be able to call on your friends.

Liebe Liesel!

Ipswich, den 21. September

Vielen Dank für Deine Karte von der Ostsee*. Es sieht ja da sehr schön aus. Hat es Dir dort gefallen? Was habt Ihr gemacht?

Ich will Dich um Rat bitten. Nächstes Jahr haben wir die Absicht, zu Ostern mit dem Auto nach Deutschland zu fahren. Wir wollen zwei Wochen an der Mosel und an dem Rhein verbringen. Was kann man da machen? Gibt es etwas Interessantes zu sehen? Was für Kleider soll man mitbringen? Wie wird das Wetter sein? Hoffentlich werden wir auch bei Euch vorbeikommen. Werdet Ihr zu dieser Zeit zu Hause sein? Bitte, schicke mir einen Stadtplan von Koblenz, damit wir Euer Haus finden können.

Ich freue mich schon auf unseren Besuch. Hoffentlich klappt es! Laß bald von Dir hören.

Viele Grüße, auch an Deine Eltern.

Deine,

Margaret.

Points to notice:
(à) Although we are writing to one friend, we sometimes mention her family and so we have to use the correct form of address.
(b) A second way of asking someone to write back soon.

*die Ostsee—*the Baltic*.

A I *Here are some of Germany's more popular holiday areas. See if you can find them on a map.*

Lüneburger Heide—moorland and nature reserve, south of Hamburg.
Eifel—highland region with quiet lakes and nature reserves north of the Mosel and west of the Rhein.
Harz—attracts walkers and winter sports enthusiasts with its cliffs, moors and lakes. South of Braunschweig.
Rhön—forest area with half-timbered buildings. Centre for gliding. Contains the baroque city of Fulda.
Odenwald—wooded mountains east of Heidelberg, with stags and wild boar.
Schwäbische Alb—south of Stuttgart, famous for stalactite caves and popular with walkers and hang-gliders.
Bayerischer Wald—between Regensburg and the Czech border.
Schwarzwald—with Baden-Baden and Freiburg, famous for its scenic beauty and spas.
Sauerland—area of mountains, caves and lakes south of the Ruhr.
Taunus—wooded mountains with Wiesbaden and its 27 hot springs.
Spessart—wooded mountains east of Frankfurt am Main.
Bodensee—lake joining Germany, Austria and Switzerland. Tropical Mainau and ancient Reichenau.
Allgäu—in the south around Immenstadt, an area of pine forests and waterfalls, with eagles, stags and deer.

II *These are the main holiday times in Germany:*

Weihnachten—*Christmas*   Ostern—*Easter*
Silvester—*New Year's Eve*   Pfingsten—*Whitsun*

B *Notice the construction* etwas Interessantes, *which means "something interesting". After* etwas *the adjective* interessant *takes a capital letter and adds* –es. *Practise with these:*

1 something nice.   2 something big.
3 something new.

C I *Practise writing a letter to Liesel about a holiday you intend to spend in Germany:*

1 Thank her for her card and say it looks nice there.
2 Ask if she liked it and what she did there.
3 Say you want to ask for advice and outline your intended holiday, saying when and where you are going.
4 Ask what you can do and see, and what sort of clothes you should bring.
5 Say you hope to call on them if they are going to be at home.
6 Ask for a town plan so that you can find their house.
7 Say you are looking forward to the visit and you hope it comes off.

II *Practise replying to a letter which Liesel has written, asking about a holiday her family intends spending in your country.*

1 Was kann man da machen?
2 Gibt es etwas Interessantes zu sehen?
3 Was für Kleider soll man mitbringen?
4 Wie wird das Wetter sein? *(Choose your own time of year)*.

10

This is a thankyou letter for a birthday present. When writing a letter like this, avoid giving a list of presents and who gave them to you, but try to say a little about them.

DANKE FÜR DAS SCHÖNE GESCHENK....

Jesmond, den 31. Oktober

Lieber Franz!

Vielen Dank für Deinen Brief, und für das Geschenk, das Du mir geschickt hast. Das Kölner Stadtwappen* wird Mutti an meinen Anorak nähen, und die komischen *Aufkleber werde ich in meinem Zimmer und an meine Schulmappe kleben.

Ich hatte andere schöne Geschenke. Von meinem Vater bekam ich ein interessantes Buch über alte Autos, und Mutti gab mir einen schönen Kugelschreiber, womit ich diesen Brief schreibe! Meine Freunde schenkten mir einige Schallplatten. Ich lud sie zum Tee ein — es gab Butterbrote, Kuchen, Torte und so weiter zu essen — und danach spielten wir die neuen Schallplatten vor. Schade, daß man Geburtstag nur einmal im Jahr hat!

Ich lege Dir einige Fußballprogramme von Newcastle United bei. Das ist meine Lieblingsmannschaft! Kannst du mir welche aus der Bundesliga schicken?

Nochmals vielen Dank. Herzliche Grüße von

Alan.

*Stadtwappen means 'coat of arms' and they often appear as presents in the form of *Anhänger* ('charms' for a bracelet) as well as badges.
*Aufkleber are 'stickers' and you can also get *Autoaufkleber* for cars.

A Germany's league football clubs are organised like this: the top league is the *Bundesliga* with 18 teams, and below that are two leagues, the *Zweite Liga Nord* and the *Zweite Liga Süd*, each of which contains 20 teams. There is promotion and relegation (three teams) between these and the *Bundesliga*. If you have a penfriend, ask him or her to send you a magazine called *Fußball-Woche*, which will give you all the news about German football.

B I *The name of any town can be used as an adjective to describe something, and the adjective ending will always be* –er. *Thus*: die Stuttgarter Zeitung; am Londoner Flughafen.

II *Notice how to say "once a year"*—einmal im Jahr. *With other times, the phrase is slightly different:*

einmal am Tag   einmal im Monat
einmal in der Woche   einmal im Jahr

C *Practise writing a thankyou letter to your penfriend:*

1 Thank him or her for the letter and the present.
2 Say why you like it, or how you will use it.
3 Describe some other presents and say who they were from.
4 Describe your birthday tea or whatever, and say what you did.
5 Say you enclose some football programmes from the club you support, and ask your penfriend if he or she can send you some in return.

This is the cover of the Stadion-Zeitung *of* Arminia Bielefeld (Zweite Liga Nord) *in their promotion decider against* 1860 München *from the* Zweite Liga Süd.

11

You would write a letter like this to say thankyou for a visit or a holiday you spent with a family. After saying you got home in one piece, mention a few things which you particularly enjoyed and any souvenirs or presents which you may have taken back with you.

ICH HABE VIELE SOUVENIRS ZURÜCKGEBRACHT.

Kendal, den 16. November

Liebe Familie Schäfer!

Am Freitagabend bin ich gut nach Hause gekommen und mein Bruder Peter hat mich vom Bahnhof abgeholt. Ich war natürlich müde nach der langen Reise aber die Überfahrt war nicht schlecht.

Ich möchte Ihnen für Ihre Gastfreundschaft danken. Die zwei Wochen, die ich bei Ihnen verbrachte, waren wirklich prima. Stuttgart fand ich sehr schön und sauber, und im Schwimmbad und im Park Killesberg kann man viel Spaß haben. Der Ausflug den Neckar hinauf nach Ludwigsburg hat mir besonders viel Freude gemacht, und das Schloß hat mir imponiert. Oben auf dem Fernsehturm war es auch ganz toll!

Ich habe viele Souvenirs zurückgebracht. Wenn meine Fotos fertig sind, werde ich Ihnen einige Abbilder schicken. Meine Eltern danken Ihnen auch für ihre Geschenke; Mutter findet den Schnaps etwas stark, aber Vater schmeckt er!

Herzliche Grüße,

Ihr

Stephen

Notice: A change in the form of address. Although this is not a formal letter, the *Sie-Sie-Ihnen-Ihr* pattern must be used when writing to a family with whom you are not on very familiar terms.

A A number of German cities have a *Fernsehturm*, from the top of which you can get a wonderful view of the surrounding area. You can also sit in the restaurant part of the way up—in some cases a revolving restaurant!

B I *Two more useful phrases to do with enjoyment are:*
Freude machen; Spaß haben *or* Spaß machen.
e.g. Der Besuch hat mir viel Freude gemacht.
     Habt ihr Spaß gehabt?
     Viel Spaß!
     "Durst macht Spaß mit Fanta!"

Practise with:
1 Das Picknick im Wald.
2 Der Ausflug nach Reichenau.
3 Im Park.
4 Die Schiffahrt nach Bingen.
5 Die Spaziergänge am See.

II *We use* den Fluß hinauf *for "up the river". "Down" is* hinunter, *used in exactly the same way. The construction is the same as with* entlang *(along)*—hinauf, hinunter *and* entlang *follow the noun, which is in the Accusative case* (den, die, das).

Practise with these:
1 down the road   5 along the street
2 along the bank   6 up the river
3 up the mountain   7 along the river
4 up the tree   8 along the coast

III *A useful group of words, particularly for describing pictures, is:* oben, unten, vorne, hinten.
     Oben links sieht man einen Vogel.
     Unten rechts steht ein Haus.
     Hinten stehen Bäume.
     Vorne sieht man einen Jungen.
Practise using these words with a picture.

C *Practise writing a thankyou letter to the Schäfer family:*

1 Tell them when you got home safely and who collected you from the station.
2 Say you were tired and that the crossing was bad.
3 Thank them for their hospitality.
4 Mention a few things which you particularly enjoyed. These could include:

der Park   der Besuch
das Schwimmbad   das Schloß
der Ausflug nach   die Läden
die Schiffahrt nach   das Essen
der Spaziergang   der Fernsehturm
   nach   der Zoo
das Picknick

5 Say you will send them some pictures when they are ready.
6 Your parents thank the family for their present(s).

12 This letter involves refusing an invitation—cancelling a previous arrangement and saying that you cannot visit the family as intended. It would be appropriate to say how disappointed you are, and that you hope you are not causing them any inconvenience.

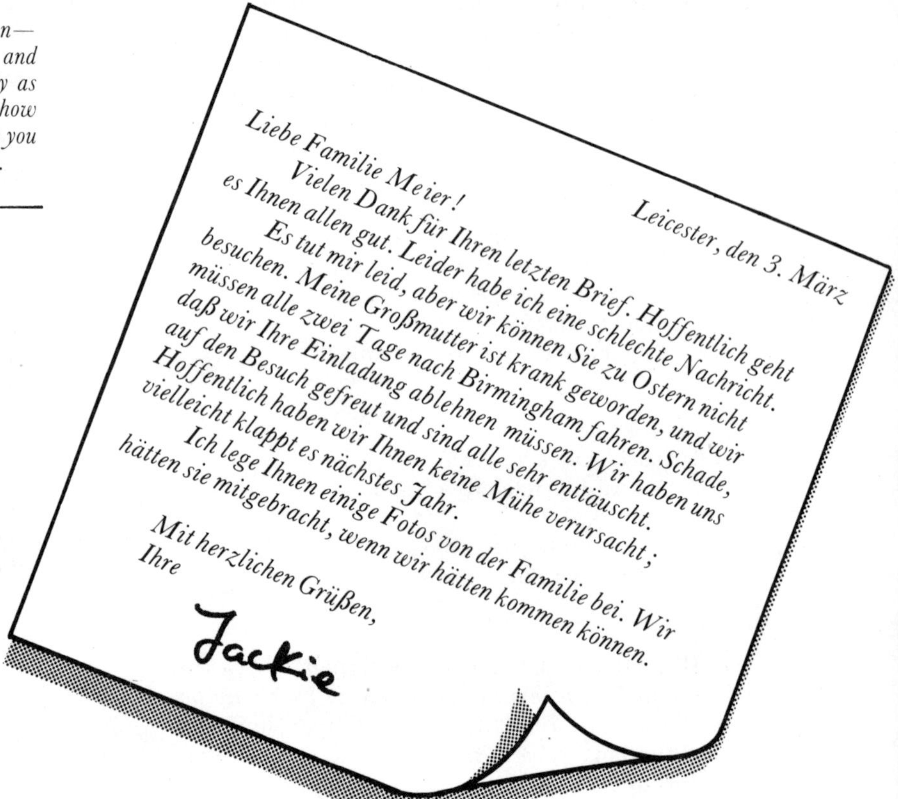

Liebe Familie Meier! Leicester, den 3. März

Vielen Dank für Ihren letzten Brief. Hoffentlich geht es Ihnen allen gut. Leider habe ich eine schlechte Nachricht. Es tut mir leid, aber wir können Sie zu Ostern nicht besuchen. Meine Großmutter ist krank geworden, und wir müssen alle zwei Tage nach Birmingham fahren. Schade, daß wir Ihre Einladung ablehnen müssen. Wir haben uns auf den Besuch gefreut und sind alle sehr enttäuscht. Hoffentlich haben wir Ihnen keine Mühe verursacht; vielleicht klappt es nächstes Jahr.

Ich lege Ihnen einige Fotos von der Familie bei. Wir hätten sie mitgebracht, wenn wir hätten kommen können.

Mit herzlichen Grüßen,
Ihre

Jackie

Points to notice:
(a) Again the formal *Sie*-form is used in an informal letter, because you do not yet count this family as close friends.
(b) A slightly different way of signing off.

A *Perhaps we should gather all your possible relatives together under one roof!*

der Vater	die Mutter
der Bruder	die Schwester
der Sohn	die Tochter
der Großvater	die Großmutter
der Enkel *(grandson)*	die Enkelin
der Onkel	die Tante
der Vetter *(male cousin)*	die Kusine *(female cousin)*
der Neffe	die Nichte *(niece)*
der Schwiegervater *(father-in-law)*	die Schwiegermutter
der Stiefvater *(stepfather)*	die Stiefmutter

das Baby, das Kind

B *Different ways of apologising:*

Es tut mir leid.
Entschuldige, entschuldigt, entschuldigen Sie.
Entschuldigung.
Verzeih, verzeiht, verzeihen Sie.
Verzeihung.
Pardon.

C I *Practise writing to the Meier family, saying why you have to cancel your proposed visit:*

1 Thank them for their letter.
2 Say you hope they are all well, but that you have bad news.
3 Say you are sorry you cannot visit them, due to illness in the family.
4 You had been looking forward to the visit and are disappointed.
5 You hope it does not give them too much trouble, and that perhaps next year the visit will come off.
6 You enclose some pictures of the family which you would have brought if you had been able to go.

II *Your penfriend has written you a letter similar to the one on page 26. Reply to it, making the following points:*

1 Thank them for the letter and the photographs.
2 Say you hope they are well.
3 You are sorry that they cannot visit you.
4 You had been looking forward to their visit and are disappointed.
5 Wish grandmother a quick recovery.
6 It will not make difficulties for you. Perhaps the visit will come off next year.

ICH HABE EINE SCHLECHTE NACHRICHT....

13 *In this letter, you wish your penfriend a happy birthday and a happy Christmas. It is an opportunity to ask how he spent his birthday, and how they celebrate Christmas. Then comes an example of how, quite simply, you can explain something of our Christmas tradition to your penfriend.*

.... WIE DU DEINEN GEBURTSTAG VERBRACHT HAST

Manchester, den 2. Dezember

Hallo Werner!

Herzliche Glückwünsche zum Geburtstag! Hoffentlich gefällt Dir das Geschenk. Sag mir, was für andere Geschenke Du bekommen hast, und wie Du Deinen Geburtstag verbracht hast.

Schade, daß Du Geburtstag so kurz vor Weihnachten hast. Bekommst Du von den Eltern ein oder zwei Geschenke? Bei uns ist das Wetter ziemlich kalt und naß; zu Weihnachten schneit es bei uns selten. Wie ist das Wetter bei Dir?

Sag mir, wie man bei Euch Weihnachten feiert. Bei uns hängen die Kinder am Heiligen Abend Strümpfe am Bettende auf. Am nächsten Morgen sind die Strümpfe voll von Geschenken, die „Father Christmas" während der Nacht bringt! Ist das bei Euch auch so?

Ich wünsche Euch allen frohe Weihnachten und ein glückliches Neues Jahr!

Dein

Andrew

Notice: A very informal way of beginning and ending a letter to a friend.

Here are some useful phrases expressing wishes:

A
1. herzliche Glückwünsche zum Geburtstag!
2. frohe Weihnachten!
3. ein fröhliches Neues Jahr/ein glückliches Neujahr/alles Gute zum neuen Jahr!
4. gute Besserung! *(after an illness)*
5. gute Reise/gute Fahrt
6. komm gut nach Hause
7. ich gratuliere zur Verlobung *(on an engagement)*
8. viel Spaß/viel Vergnügen
9. viel Glück!
10. alles Gute!

B *A phrase like* bei dir *can mean: "at your house", "where you live", "in your town" (or country), and so on depending on context.*
Practise the construction with these:

1. at his house.
2. where I live.
3. at her house.
4. in your country. (a) friend; (b) friends; (c) stranger.
5. where we live.
6. at Schäfers' house.

C I *Practise writing a letter to Werner, wishing him a happy birthday:*

1. Wish him a happy birthday, and say you hope he likes his present.
2. Ask him to tell you what other presents he had, and how he spent his birthday.
3. Say what the weather is like, and ask what it is like where he lives.

II *Now write to Ulrike, wishing her a happy Christmas:*

1. Wish her a happy Christmas, and say you hope she likes her present.
2. Ask her what other presents she had, and how Christmas is celebrated where she lives.
3. Describe how Christmas is celebrated in England.
4. Say what the weather is like, and ask what it is like where she lives.
5. Wish the family a happy New Year.

III *Werner has written to you on your birthday. Answer his questions:*

1. Was für andere Geschenke hast du bekommen?
2. Wie hast du deinen Geburtstag verbracht?
3. Wie ist das Wetter bei dir?

IV *Ulrike has written to you at Christmas. Answer her questions:*

1. Wie ist das Wetter bei dir?
2. Was für Geschenke hast du bekommen?
3. Sag mir, wie man bei dir Weihnachten feiert.

14 FORMAL LETTERS

This is the first of the formal letters, written to someone you have never seen before. Here you are requesting information from the officials of the Verkehrsamt *(Tourist Office) in the area where you intend to spend your holidays.*

Nottingham, den 10. Juni

An das Verkehrsamt,
555 Bernkastel-Kues,
Gestade 6.

Sehr geehrte Herren!
    Meine Familie und ich haben die Absicht, unsere Ferien in Bernkastel zu verbringen, und ich möchte Sie um Auskunft bitten.
    Wir haben einen Platz vom 7. bis zum 28. August auf dem Campingplatz „Schenk" reserviert. Ich möchte gerne wissen, was es zu dieser Zeit in Bernkastel und der Umgebung zu sehen und zu tun gibt.
    Ich wäre sehr dankbar, wenn Sie mir auch einen Stadtplan schicken könnten.
    Hochachtungsvoll,
George Williams

A   Usually in German addresses, the town comes directly after the name of the person or place you are writing to. Then come the house number and street name, although this is now gradually changing to the order we use in Britain.
The number in front of the town—the *Postleitzahl*—is very important and should always be included. The size of the town can be seen from the number of figures in the *Postleitzahl*. 7 (or 7000) Stuttgart is bigger than 48 (or 4800) Bielefeld, which in turn is bigger than 798 (or 7980) Ravensburg.

B   We use the phrase die Absicht haben *for "to intend". It is followed by an infinitive with* zu.
Practise using this construction to say that you intend spending your holidays in the following places:

1 am Bodensee   2 in Koblenz   3 im Schwarzwald
4 im Taunus   5 an der Mosel

C   *Practise writing to a tourist office asking for information:*

1 Say you intend spending your holiday in Lindau and would like to ask for information.
2 You have reserved a site from August 1st–14th.
3 You would like to know what there is to see and do in and around Lindau at this time.
4 You would be grateful if they would send you a town plan.

Points to notice:
(a) In a formal letter, the name and address of the people you are writing to appear at the top left hand side.
(b) Always use the *Sie-Sie-Ihnen-Ihr* pattern, and you can always sign off with *Hochachtungsvoll*.
(c) When you are not writing to any one person in particular, begin with "Dear Sirs": *Sehr geehrte Herren!*

A letter on these lines will easily reserve what accommodation you want in a hotel. It also states the most you are prepared to pay for one night; this is useful for the management to reserve for you the kind of room you want. It also asks them to recommend somewhere else if they are full.

> Oxford, den 18. Mai
>
> An die Direktion,
> Hotel am Zoo,
> 1 Berlin,
> Kurfürstendamm 25.
>
> Sehr geehrte Herren!
>   Hiermit bitte ich Sie, mir für die Zeit vom 25. Juli bis zum 7. August ein Doppelzimmer mit Dusche zu reservieren. Ich möchte höchstens DM 50.00 pro Nacht bezahlen.
>   Falls das nicht möglich ist, wäre ich Ihnen sehr dankbar, wenn Sie mir ein anderes Hotel in der Nähe empfehlen könnten.
>   Hochachtungsvoll,
>   *Alan Randall*

Notice: Letters of this kind often begin with *hiermit*. See which others do.

A *You can practise reserving what accommodation you need by using this table:*

ein	Einzelzimmer	mit	Bad
zwei	Doppelzimmer		Dusche
			fließendem Wasser

B *Practise the opening of a letter like this by booking the following accommodation on these dates:*

1. single room with bath, August 1–3.
2. single room with shower, July 4–11.
3. double room with shower, May 6–14.
4. double room and single room with shower, June 1–8.
5. two single rooms with bath, October 25–30.

C *Now write these letters asking for rooms at the* Hotel Teutoburger Wald, 48 Bielefeld, Detmolder Straße.

1. You would like a single room with a shower, July 15–20, not more than DM 40.00 per night, or can they recommend another.
2. You would like suitable accommodation for your family, July 28–August 2, not more than DM 50.00 per night, or can they recommend another.

In this letter you reserve a site for a tent or a caravan on a camp-site. Obviously they need to know the dates of your stay and also the ages of the people involved, so that they can work out the cost, as you ask. You also ask for information about facilities on and near the site.

Poole, den 12. April

An die Verwaltung
des Campingplatzes ,,Schenk'',
555 Bernkastel-Kues.

Sehr geehrte Herren!

Hiermit bitte ich Sie, mir einen Platz für ein Zelt zu reservieren, und zwar vom 3. bis 9. eventuell 10. Juli. Wir sind zwei Personen im Alter von 18 Jahren. Ich möchte wissen, was es kosten wird.
Bitte teilen Sie mir auch mit, ob ein Schwimmbad beziehungsweise Tennisplatz in der Nähe von dem Campingplatz ist.

Hochachtungsvoll,

David Shepherd

Points to notice:
(a) *und zwar* is used again because we are specifying dates.
(b) *eventuell* is often used to mean "possibly", "if necessary".
(c) *beziehungsweise* means "or", "respectively", and is a little more professional than *oder*.
(d) The same letter could equally well be used to book a place on a caravan site—*einen Platz für einen Wohnwagen.*

A I It is always advisable to book in advance at a campsite in Germany. You will have to pay for your site and also for the number of people in your party. There is a reduction for children. The site is almost certain to be equipped with laundry facilities and a shop, but there is no harm in asking to make sure.

II *You will find the following table useful in giving details about how many people are in your group:*

Wir sind	zwei Erwachsene drei Erwachsene vier Erwachsene	und	ein Kind. zwei Kinder. keine Kinder.

B I *You can use this sentence pattern to ask about facilities near the site:*

Bitte teilen Sie mir auch mit, ob . . . beziehungsweise . . . in der Nähe von dem Campingplatz ist.

Here are some facilities you may need to ask about:

das Postamt—*post office*
das Kino—*cinema*
der Kinderspielplatz—*playground*
das Schwimmbad—*swimming pool*
die Läden—*shops*
die Apotheke—*chemist*

Now ask about:
1 swimming pool or alternatively a cinema.
2 shops or alternatively a chemist.
3 playground or alternatively a cinema.
4 post office or alternatively shops.

II *You can use a similar pattern to ask about facilities on the site:*

Bitte teilen Sie mir auch mit, ob . . . und . . . auf dem Campingplatz sind.

And some facilities you could inquire about:

Duschen—*showers*
ein Lebensmittelgeschäft—*food shop*
der Parkplatz—*car park*
die Waschangelegenheiten—*washing facilities*
das Telefon—*telephone*
ob in der Nähe Autos zu vermieten sind—*if cars can be hired nearby.*

Use a few of them to practise as before.

C I *Practise booking a site for a tent, using the following outlines:*

(a) One tent. July 27 to 30 or possibly 31. Two adults. How much? Are there showers and a shop on the site?

(b) One tent. August 17 to 24 or possibly 25. Two adults and a child of eight. How much? Are there washing facilities and showers on the site?

II *Practise booking a site for your caravan, using these outlines:*

(a) June 14 to 18. Two adults and a child of nine. How much? Is there a playground or a cinema near the site?

(b) Reserve a site for your family on a caravan holiday. Choose your own dates, give details of your family as shown, and ask how much it will cost. Inquire about any other facilities to suit your family, on or near the camp site.

In this letter to a youth hostel, you reserve beds and linen, and enquire about meals. It also contains a useful way of asking for an early answer.

Stoke-on-Trent, den 3. Mai

An den Herbergsvater*,
*DJH Landshut,
555 Bernkastel.

Sehr geehrter Herr!

Ich möchte hiermit zwei Betten für den 20. und 21. eventuell 22. Juni reservieren, und zwar für zwei sechzehnjährige Jungen. Wir möchten auch Bettlaken und Kopfkissen entleihen — Schlafsäcke haben wir schon. Wäre es möglich, Frühstück und Abendessen im Hause zu haben? Ich bitte Sie höflichst um eine baldige Antwort.

Hochachtungsvoll,

Gary Mason

---

*Herbergsvater — *Youth Hostel warden.*
*DJH = Deutsche Jugendherbergen — *German Youth Hostel Association.*

A German youth hostels will hire out bed linen to visitors, but it is usual to provide your own sleeping-bag. If you do not have one, you can hire that as well.
Look on the notice-board (*das Schwarze Brett* or *die Anschlagtafel*) for the daily routine and rules (*die Hausordnung*).
You should be able to find the hostel easily enough by following the triangular DJH signs, so there is no need to write and ask for directions. If in doubt, ask someone: "*Wie komme ich zu der Jugendherberge, bitte?*"

B *Practise booking accommodation in a youth hostel, for:*

1 two girls; 17 years old; June 15–19; linen required; breakfast required; quick reply.

2 three boys; 15 years old; August 22 and possibly 23; linen and pillows required; evening meal and breakfast required; quick reply.

3 yourself; how old; July 2 and 3, possibly also 4; linen and pillow required; breakfast and evening meal required; quick reply.

Notice: Although you don't know him, you are writing this time to one specific person (the *Herbergsvater*) and so begin with "Dear Sir" rather than "Dear Sirs".

18 *In this letter you reply to an advertisement. You apply for a job and give a few details about yourself, rather like you did in your first letters to a penfriend. You also enclose a reference and a copy of your school report.*

Trowbridge, den 17. März

An die
Zentralstelle für Arbeitsvermittlung,
Central Placement Office,
6 FRANKFURT AM MAIN,
Feuerbachstraße 42.

Betrifft: Angebot in der "Daily Telegraph" vom 15. März

Sehr geehrte Herren!
 Hiermit möchte ich mich bei Ihnen als Au-Pair Mädchen bewerben*.
 Ich heiße June Margaret Wilson und bin Engländerin. Meine Adresse ist: 7 Church Road, Trowbridge, Wiltshire. Ich bin am 2. Oktober 1961 in Trowbridge geboren. Ich bin Schulabgängerin, natürlich ledig und möchte ein Jahr bei einer deutschen Familie verbringen, um meine Deutschkenntnisse zu erweitern, bevor ich weiterstudiere. Ich lerne Deutsch seit drei Jahren und habe meine O-level Prüfungen gemacht.
 Ich füge einen Empfehlungsbrief und eine Zeugnisabschrift von der Schule bei.
 Hochachtungsvoll,

June Wilson

Points to notice:
(a) State the business of the letter at the top by introducing it with *Betrifft* ("concerning").
(b) *beifügen* is a more formal way of saying "to enclose" than *beilegen*.

*sich bewerben—*to apply (for a job, etc.).*

A I *If you are interested in finding a position as an Au Pair, or in finding a holiday job, you should write to:*

> Zentralstelle für Arbeitsvermittlung,
> Central Placement Office,
> 6 Frankfurt am Main,
> Feuerbachstraße 42.

or Verein für Internationale Jugendarbeit e. V.
6 Frankfurt am Main,
Gutleutstraße 45.

You should send the following particulars:

Surname and all Christian names
Nationality
Permanent address in the U.K.
Date and place of birth
Marital Status
Number of dependent children, if any
Professional and vocational training
Present occupation
How well you know the German language
Nature and duration of desired occupation in Germany
Whether you are coming alone or with family.

Here are some phrases and vocabulary which you will find useful for giving some of the particulars:

Engländer/in; Waliser/in; Schotte/Schottin; Irländer/in.
Ich bin am 5. August 1957 in London geboren.
Ich bin verheiratet/ledig/geschieden. *(married/single/divorced)*
Ich bin Schulabgänger/in; Student/in.
Ich studiere Deutsch seit vier Jahren.

Ich möchte sechs Monate/ein Jahr in Deutschland verbringen.

The others will have been covered earlier, or will not apply to you.

II *You will need to know this vocabulary when reading advertisements for jobs in the* Stellenanzeigen *page of a newspaper:*

der Lebenslauf—*curriculum vitae*
das Angebot (e)—*offer*
die Unterlagen—*particulars*
die Offerte (n)—*offer*
das Lichtbild—*photograph*
die Zeugnisabschrift (en)—*copy of certificate*
die Gehaltsvorstellung (en)—*salary requirement*
die Bewerbung—*application*
erbeten—*requested*
der Empfehlungsbrief—*reference*

B *You will find useful a phrase we used in letter 6:* ich interessiere mich für *(I am interested in). Combine this phrase with:*

> das Theater—*the theatre*
> Kinder—*children*
> Tiere—*animals*
> Maschinen—*machines*

and say:

(a) I am interested in the theatre.
(b) I am interested in children.
(c) I am interested in animals.
(d) I am interested in machines.

C I *Now look at these job advertisements from a newspaper. Make up your own dates and write letters of application for the jobs advertised at:*

    (a) Das Zimmertheater.
    (b) Hermann Rabe KG.
    (c) Das Tierheim des Tierschutzvereins Münster/Westfalen.

Follow the pattern of the model letter. Give your name, age, address, say you are a school-leaver and what you are interested in (Section B). Enclose a reference and a copy of your school report.

II *Read the other job advertisements. Write an application for one of them following exactly the lines shown, and giving whatever details the employer requires.*

STELLENANZEIGEN

Büromaschinen-Mechaniker zum baldmöglichen Eintritt gesucht. Hermann Rabe KG, Büromaschinen, 44 Münster.

Hilfskraft für Tierheim (weibl.), vormittags, sofort gesucht. Tierheim des Tierschutzvereins Münster Westf. und Umgebung e. V., Dingstiege 71. Ruf 3 22 80

Das **Zimmertheater** sucht zum 1. 9. 77 einen neuen jungen flexiblen Mann für Bühnenarbeiten.

Dringend gesucht! **Kinderfrau** in Dauerstellung für 2 Kinder (3 und 5) montags bis freitags 7.30 Uhr bis 13 Uhr, von Lehrerin Münster-Gelmer, Tel. 3 23 19

DM 1800,– bis 2800,–
FREMDSPRACHEN-
SEKRETÄRINNEN
BUCHHALTERINNEN
STENOTYPISTINNEN
KONTORISTINNEN
LOCHERINNEN
für sofort oder später auch zur Aushilfe gesucht. Greifen Sie z. Tel. **econoMARK**, 6 Frankfurt, Zeil 81. Telefon 06 11 / 28 39 54

Handelsschülerin/Abiturientin
als Sachbearbeiterin f. unser Reedereikontor, findet interessante, vielseitige Tätigkeit in einem internat. Unternehmen. Auch Anfäng. Neben einem marktgerechten Gehalt, div. sozialen Leistungen bieten wir ein gutes Arbeitsklima i. einem jungen Team. Rufen Sie uns an. **Karl Geuther & Co., 6 Ffm,** Telefon 06 11 / 2 07 57

? Was bin ich ?
Verkäuferin? Kassiererin? Friseuse? Servierin? Ausländerin? Arbeiterin? Büroangestellte? Schulabgängerin? Egal, was Sie heute sind. In vier Wochen erlernen Sie abends nach der Arbeit oder nachmittags den Beruf der **IBM-LOCHERIN/DATENTYPISTIN**, Karte/Diskette. Ohne Vorkenntnisse. **KEIN VERDIENSTAUSFALL.**
Endlich gibt es den Beruf mit der vernünftigen Arbeitszeit. Es gibt die Ganztagsarbeit, die Halbtagsarbeit, die Wochenendarbeit, die Studenarbeit, die Abendarbeit und die Heimarbeit.

Hessen horcht auf DM 1900,– monatlich und mehr kann eine gute Locherin verdienen.
Werden auch Sie IBM-Locherin ohne Vorkenntnisse. In vier Wochen schon können Sie als Locherin arbeiten.
SPRECH- und BERATUNGSSTUNDEN NUR DONNERSTAG, 18. AUGUST 1977, VON 10.00 BIS 19.30 UHR. Minderjährige bringen Erziehungsberechtigte mit. Kommen Sie zu uns! Der Weg lohnt sich immer.
Locherinnen-Schule, 6 Frankfurt, Hasengasse 25, Eing. Holzgraben 1 A

Interviewer

für Marktforschungsumfragen gesucht. Sie sollten viel freie Zeit haben und auch mal für mehrere Tage in einer anderen Stadt interviewen können.

Schriftliche Bewerbungen an

FIELD RESEARCH
Markt- und Meinungsforschung
Bernhard Schreiber
4402 Greven
Ludw.-Terfloth-Straße 42

Junge aufgeschlossene
Kosmetikerin
zum 1. 10. 1977 gesucht.

Parfümerie La Femme
6236 Eschborn, Schwalbacher Straße 18, Tel. 0 61 96 / 4 17 16

WYETH
Unser Erfolg Ihre Chance
Wyeth stellt noch einen männlichen
AUSZU-BILDENDEN
ein.

Voraussetzung: Abschluß der mittleren Reife oder Abschluß der höheren Handelsschule.

Schriftliche Bewerbungen (letztes Schulzeugnis, Lebenslauf, Lichtbild) sind zu richten an die Personalabteilung.

WYETH PHARMA GMBH

Drogistin oder Parfümerie-Verkäuferin

zum 1. Oktober 1977 gesucht.

Drogerie und Parfümerie
Otto Krumbein
Inh. Elfriede Krumbein
Münster, Bahnhofstr. 4
Telefon 4 51 71

Biete Ausbildungsplatz:
Auszubildende
im hauswirtschaftlichen Bereich für zwei Jahre gesucht.

Abschluß: Hauswirtschafterin
Unterkunft und Verpflegung im Haus, übliche Bezahlung.

Franz-Hitze-Haus, Kardinal-von-Galen-Ring 50, Münster
Telefon 8 00 31 — Hausverwaltung: Müller

Here is an example of the kind of letter which could have been written by someone answering this advertisement:

Wyeth Pharma GMBH,
44 Münster,
Schleebrüggenkamp 15.

Klaus Meier,
44 Münster,
Hansaplatz 4.
Münster
den 5. Oktober 1977

Sehr geehrte Herren!

Unter Bezugnahme auf Ihre Anzeige vom Sonnabend, 3.10.1977 in der Westfälischen Zeitung, möchte ich mich um den Platz des Auszubildenden in Ihrer Firma bewerben.

Dieser Bewerbung lege ich mein letztes Schulzeugnis, einen handgeschriebenen Lebenslauf, sowie ein Lichtbild bei. Sollten Sie Wert auf eine persönliche Vorstellung legen, bitte ich Sie, mir Nachricht zu geben an die oben genannte Adresse.

Hochachtungsvoll,

Klaus Meier

Notice:
unter Bezugnahme auf — with reference to; der/die Auszubildende = trainee; einschließen = to enclose.

EXAMINATION PRACTICE

Finally, here are some questions taken from past examination papers for you to try.

1. Your teacher has arranged for you to go on an exchange trip to Germany to replace a schoolfriend who has fallen ill at the last moment. Write a letter to your exchange partner introducing yourself, explaining the situation, confirming the dates suggested and saying something about your interests, your family, your home, etc. *(about 150 words)*.

   (Cambridge, Summer 1974)

2. You have been on holiday in Germany and have left something behind at the hotel where you were staying. Write to the manager, giving the dates of the holiday, describing the article lost, saying where you think you left it and asking him to send it on to you. *(about 120 words)*

   (South-East Regional C.S.E., Summer 1976)

3. You have just returned from spending your Easter holiday with the family of your German penfriend. Write a letter to his (or her) mother thanking her for her hospitality, referring to those things you particularly enjoyed. Describe briefly the return journey from Germany and end with some mention of life now that you are back home. *(about 120 words)*

   (South-East Regional C.S.E., Summer 1976)

4. You have just left school and want to work in Germany for a while. Write a letter to your penfriend's father who is a farmer, explaining the situation. Tell him you only need to earn some pocket money; suggest when you would like to stay and how you intend to travel. *(130–150 words)*

   (Cambridge, Summer 1976)

5. Ihre Familie möchte zwei Wochen in einer Stadt im Schwarzwald verbringen. Schreiben Sie an ein Hotel, das Freunde empfohlen haben, um Zimmer zu bestellen. Fragen Sie auch über Sehenswürdigkeiten in der Stadt und Ausflüge in der Umgebung! *(140–150 words)*

   (Joint Matriculation Board 1975)

6. Write a reply to the following advertisement: „Wollen Sie uns in den Sommerferien in einem Kinderheim oder auf einem Bauernhof helfen? Schreiben Sie an Helmut Berger, Kinderheim Rosenhof, Villingen." *(140–160 words)*

   (Joint Matriculation Board 1976)

7. Sie haben einen guten Freund eingeladen, eine Woche bei Ihnen zu bleiben, und zwar vom 24. bis zum 31. August. Leider finden Sie jetzt, daß diese Woche für Sie nicht mehr möglich ist. Sie schreiben also an ihn, um sich zu entschuldigen, ihm die Sache zu erklären und seinen Besuch für später zu arrangieren. *(about 100 words)*

   (A.E.B. November 1976)

8. Sie sind für 14 Tage in die Ferien gefahren und sind jetzt seit 24 Stunden in dem Ort, wo Sie die 14 Tage verbringen wollen. Schreiben Sie an Ihre Eltern, wie es Ihnen dort gefällt! *(about 100 words)*

   (A.E.B. Summer 1976)

9 Sie wohnen in Frankfurt, und Ihre Eltern wohnen 150 Kilometer von Frankfurt entfernt. Sie bekommen den folgenden Brief von einer Tante, die seit Jahren in Amerika gelebt hat. Schreiben Sie eine passende Antwort darauf! *(about 100 words)*

(A.E.B. Summer 1976)

Lieber Christoph!

Ich freue mich auf meinen Deutschlandbesuch. Ich werde am 8. 7. mit dem Flug Nr. 265 um 06.40 in Frankfurt ankommen. Du holst mich ab, ja? Wenn Du aber willst, kann ich mit einem späteren Flug kommen.

Sag mir doch bitte, wie ich Dich erkennen kann: Du warst ein Baby, als ich Dich zuletzt sah!

Ich habe Dich in meinem ersten Brief nicht gefragt, ob Du ein eigenes Auto hast. Wenn nicht, kannst Du mich ruhig mit dem Taxi abholen; ich werde es Dir natürlich bezahlen. Deine Mutter meinte, ich würde 2 Tage bei Dir in Frankfurt bleiben und dann zu ihr fahren. Wie lange dauert die Fahrt dahin? Ich möchte unterwegs Deine Tante Irmgard besuchen, aber ich weiß nicht mehr genau, wo sie jetzt wohnt. Du mußt mir also sagen, ob man leicht dahin kommen kann.

Ich möchte Deiner Mutter ein Geschenk mitbringen. Was meinst Du, was ihr Freude machen würde?

Und zum Schluß noch: was für ein Wetter kann man im Juli bei Euch erwarten? Ist das eine dumme Frage?

Herzlichste Grüße!
Deine
Tante Hannelore